My Holy Quran Teaches Me
Introducing the Holy Quran to Muslim Children

By The Sincere Seeker Kids Collection

Oh no! Today is a stormy, gloomy day. Papa Bear and I are supposed to go fishing. It's okay, I thought to myself as I watch the raindrops race across my window.

I make smiley faces in my window with my finger. Today will be a good day even though the clouds are dark and heavy, and the rain is falling hard.

Suddenly, the power shuts off. Papa bear grabs a candle from the cupboard.

Papa Bear reaches for a beautiful dark green book from the highest shelf. "I will introduce you to a beautiful book, like no other!" he says.

"This is the Holy Quran, Baby Bear," says Papa Bear.

"What is the Holy Quran?" I ask him with a curious look on my face. "The Holy Quran is our Creator's words! Allah speaks to us, telling us what we should and should not do!' said Papa Bear.

I sat there on the ground with my legs crossed, curious to know what Allah wants to tell us. Papa Bear flips through the Holy Quran and finally lands on a page.

"Baby Bear, the Holy Quran teaches us that Allah created us and this whole world and everything in it. He is the only One we should worship," says Papa bear.

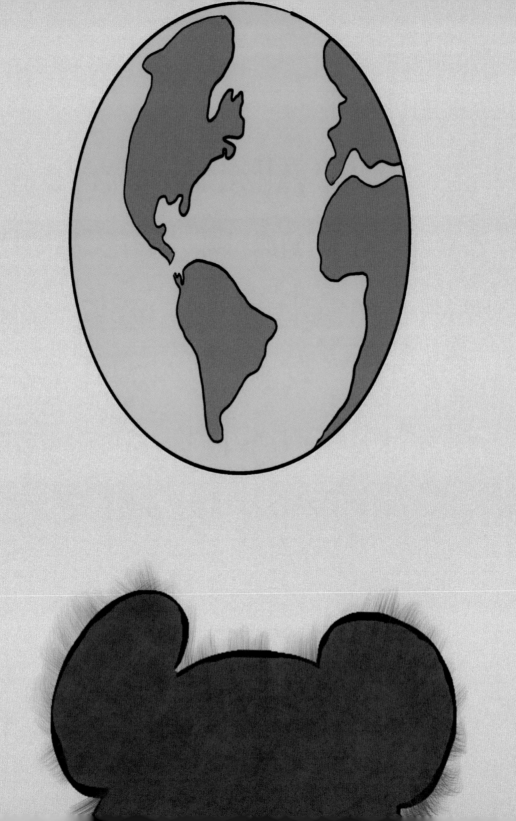

"Did Allah create everything in this world by Himself?" I ask Papa Bear. "Yes, Baby Bear, that is right!" answers Papa Bear.

As Papa Bear flips through the Holy Quran to teach me more about the Holy Quran and Allah, we hear the storm get louder and stronger. "Son, we might not be able to go out today, but that's okay because you are going to learn a lot!" he says.

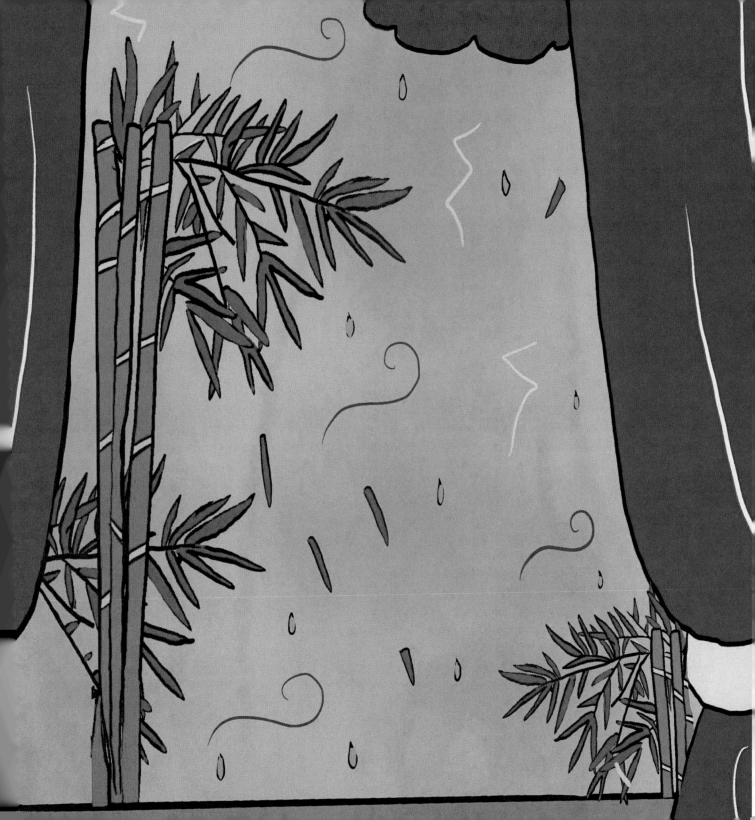

"The Holy Quran teaches us to listen to Allah and our parents," explains Papa Bear. "It teaches us that we should be kind and polite to everyone and use good words," he adds.

"The Holy Quran teaches us to help other bears that do not have as much as we do. We can help give them food like fish, berries, grains, and honey, as well as money and our time!" Papa Bear says.

"The Holy Quran teaches us that Allah loves and takes care of us, and we should love Him back," instructs Papa Bear.

"The Holy Quran teaches us not to lie, say bad words, cheat, or hurt anyone!" says Papa Bear.

No lying   No bad words

No cheating

"The Holy Quran teaches us that we should be thankful and say Alhamdulillah for everything Allah has given us. We thank our Creator and praise Him!" says Papa Bear joyfully.

"The Holy Quran teaches us to be patient during tough times and not get angry or lose hope!" Papa bear informs me.

The lights began to flicker. Suddenly, the wind calms, and the rain stops.

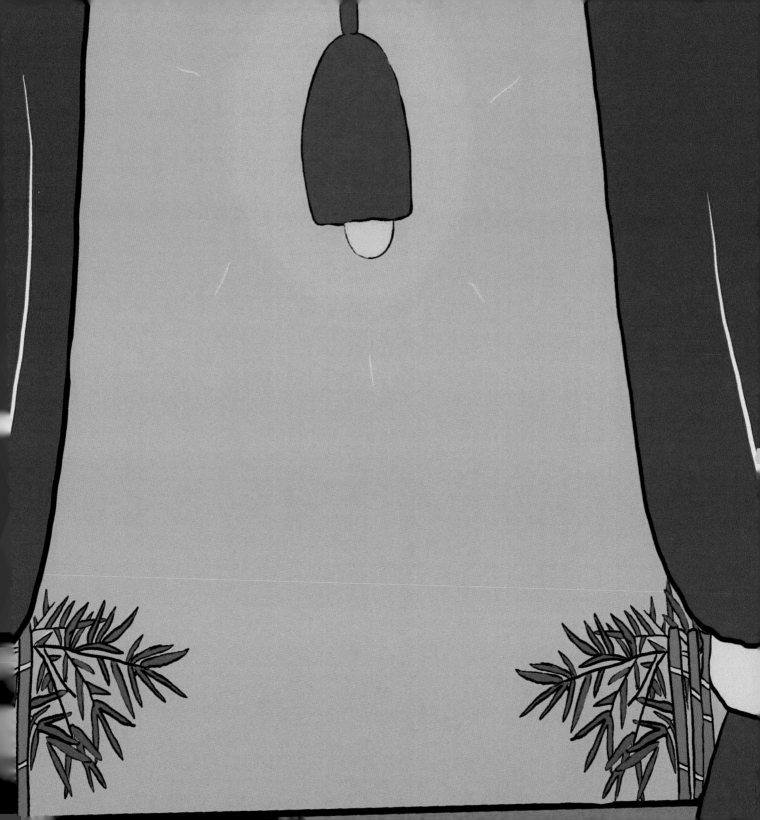

"Look outside, Papa Bear!" I scream in excitement as I point out to the window. A beautiful, colorful rainbow peaks through the clouds. "*Alhamdulliah!*" he announces.

The rain has stopped, the sun is shining, and our lights are back on! "Maybe we can go outside after all. Do you want to go fishing?' We can still go fishing now!" says Papa Bear to my delight.

I run upstairs to my room to get my fishing rod. "Ready, ready, READY!!" I scream in excitement.

The End.

Made in United States
Orlando, FL
13 March 2023

30998224R00024